Machines at the station

Henry Pluckrose

Blackwell Education

First published 1990

Basil Blackwell Ltd
108 Cowley Road
Oxford OX4 1JF
UK

British Library Cataloguing in Publication Data
Pluckrose, Henry–*1931*
1. Machinery
I. Title   II. Series
621.8

ISBN 0–631–90321–6
ISBN 0–631–16552–5 v.5

Illustrated by Peter Kent
Typeset in 20 on 30 pt Century by Columns of Reading
Printed and bound in Great Britain by MacLehose & Partners, Portsmouth.

Contents

If you go to a railway station you will see many machines.

The biggest machines of all are the
engines which pull the trains.
The engines are also called power units.

There are many kinds of engines.
Some use electricity.

This engine gets its power from the electric wires above it.

The wires go all along the track.

This engine gets electric power from a metal rail that runs along the track.

This is a very powerful engine.
It is a diesel locomotive.

It uses diesel oil to drive a generator.
The generator makes electricity.
The electricity works the engine.
This train can go 125 miles an hour.

A steam locomotive pulls this train.

The engine burns coal to heat water.
The hot water makes steam.
The power of the steam makes the wheels turn on the track.

Trains need special wheels to run on a track.

Look at the wheels of this train.

How are they different from the wheels of a car?

This train does not need a driver.
A computer does the driving.

Before you travel on a train you
must buy a ticket.

You can buy a ticket from a machine.
You push the button to tell the
machine where you want to go.
You put money in the machine and
the ticket comes out.

If you want to catch a train you need to know the platform number.

The departure board is a machine that can tell you.

If you have bags it is easy to carry them on a trolley.

A trolley is a kind of machine.
Who gives it the power to move?

Trains also carry parcels and packets.
This engine pulls its own little train of trucks.

How many machines can you find at your railway station?

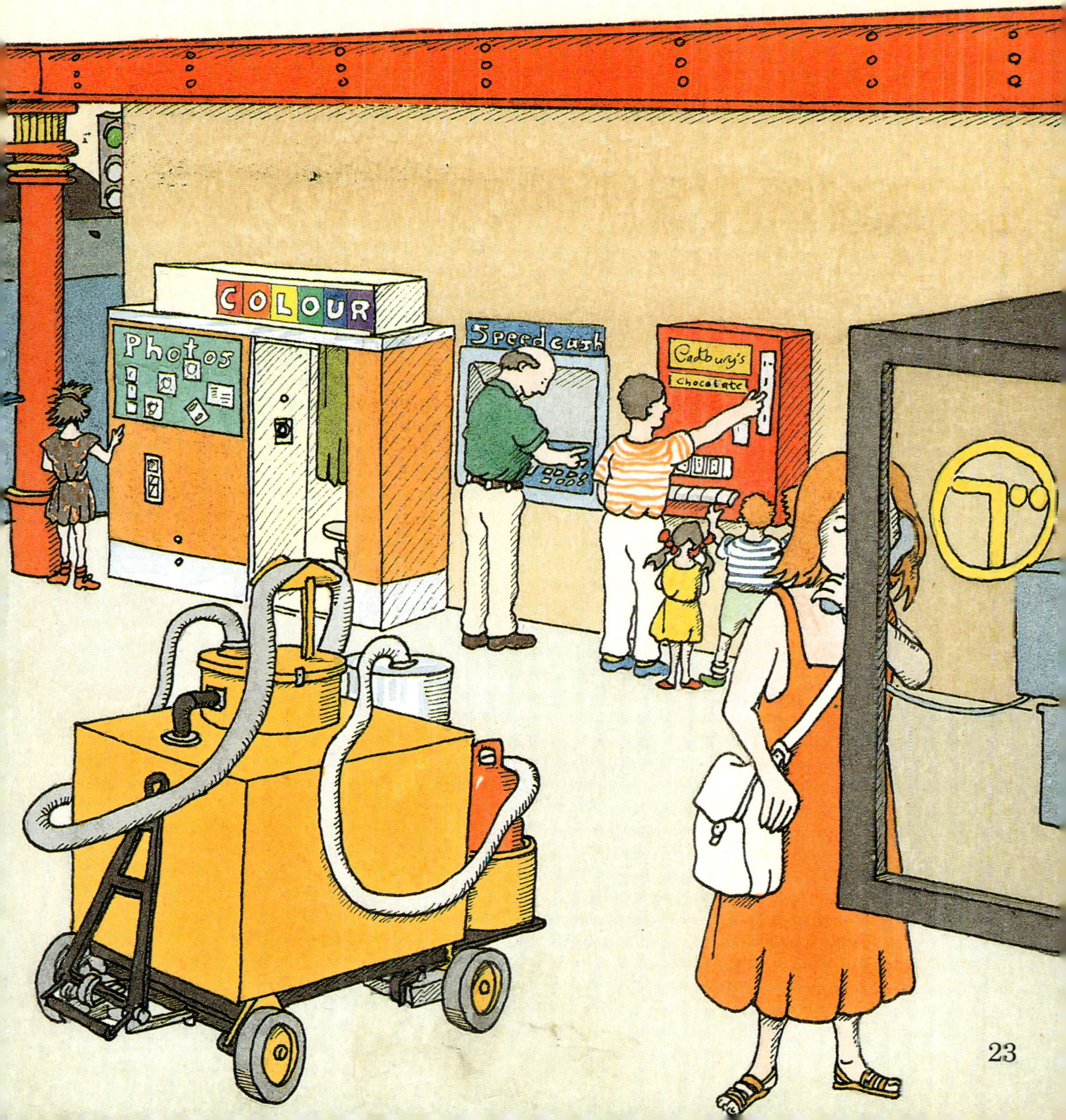

Index